DETOURS

ENJOYING THE SCENERY
ALONG THE DETOURS

ERIC
BENNETT

DETOURS

By Eric Bennett

ISBN: 978-1-60416-668-2

GNT

24 HOUR Books
On-Demand Publishing
14 S. Queen Street, Mt. Sterling, KY 40353
Orders 1-800-765-2464 | Information 859-520-3757
Fax 859-520-3757 | Text 606-359-2064
Email orders@24hourbooks.co | www.24HourBooks.co

Place your order today on Amazon!

This book is intended to be both serious and entertaining. My goal was to share a portion of scripture that will encourage someone going through a difficult season in their life.

"To every thing there is a season, and a time to every purpose under the heaven:"

Ecclesiastes 3:1 KJV

Remember that whatever you're going through is just for a season. This too shall pass. Another season will soon appear. Be encouraged!

I also wanted to include some of my own personal stories, the fun, and the struggles.

Thanks to my beautiful, incredible wife, Dana,
who is also a super mom! I love you!

To our daughter, Erin and our son Zac,
you are truly a blessing from the Lord.

Zac, thanks for your help and insight
in writing this book.

I want to thank my family for allowing
me to share some family "stuff."

Also, thank you to all my immediate family and
extended family for making life easy and fun.

I love you all!

FOREWORD

Eric Bennett's book is both uplifting and interesting. His application of Philippians 4 to real life using humorous personal illustrations was refreshing. This is a must read for anyone who has taken a detour and needs to get back on track.

Dr. Daniel J. Tyler, President
International Seminary

I am always delighted when I have the opportunity to introduce a "friend" to others. Especially when that person is more than just someone you know, but someone that you respect and hold in high esteem. It is that scenario that sets the tone of this foreword. Eric Bennett is that person.... and my friend.

As a minister and singer, Eric traverses each area of his life with dignity and expertise that sets him apart. As a singer, he navigates the lower register of his genre of music with such ease, as in the song, "Look for Me for I Will Be There Too," until we can hardly wait for that day to come true. His velvet smoothness and quality captures singers, orators, and audiences. That is why he has been chosen as "Favorite Bass" and tops in his field.

As a minister, Eric is never satisfied

until "all truth" has been discovered and exposed. He constantly continues his quest for knowledge and Biblical explanations with a willingness to listen and share dialogue, as you will learn as you read his book.

As emcee for the "nationally acclaimed" group, Triumphant, he can set his audience at ease with a humorous event or story with such subtlety, never uproariously, that the songs and message flow with liquidity. His smile and chuckle prepares any audience to enjoy the moment.

In this book, Eric carries us interestingly through warm and tender family events, and then, with equal grace, he shares with us his breadth of wisdom gained from his reading and research.

As you browse each page you will readily learn that Eric has designed each story and scripture to guide us in our relationship with Jesus Christ. May God continue to bless this anointed man, and may He bless us as we follow.

Jerry Goff, PhD, President Sharing
Christ Ministries President-Emeritus
SGMA Hall of Fame

PREFACE

My motivation and inspiration for writing this book was Randy Wright. Randy was one of my favorite people. He was the pastor of Piney Grove Baptist Church, and I have been singing at his church at least once a year for many years. He loved gospel music as much or more than anyone I have ever met. He was a collector of it. Every time we were there, he would take me back in his office and play me an old Statesmen song or

Blackwood song that had recently come to his mind. His office was filled with many albums but also many books and Bibles.

We would sit and talk about our favorite preachers and many times we would share sermon ideas. I will never forget the last time I saw him in person. I walked into his new office and sat down across from him. The church had just finished the new building and his new office was grand. I asked, "Randy, do you have any really good sermons?" He said, "I thought you'd never ask." He couldn't wait to slide his new sermon across the desk at me to see what I thought. It was only the outline but it was the outline of the book you are reading now. You see, Randy was experiencing a *detour* in his life.

Six and a half years before this conversation with him, the doctors had diagnosed him with pancreatic cancer with liver massed (that means there's not a place on his liver that doesn't have cancer on it). Incurable. Inoperable.

His gall bladder had already been removed so he had to have five surgeries to clean the toxins from his body. He had been on chemo and radiation. The last sixteen months he had been on a chemo pill daily. "This is my last hope," he said. When Randy and I met, he weighed 170lbs and wasn't fat. But this time, as I sat across from him, he told me he now weighed around 119lbs.

My friend Randy passed away at the age of 55.

INTRODUCTION

Most people have plans for their lives, either things they want to accomplish, a lifestyle they want to pursue, or at least dreams of how they think life should be. Like going on a trip, we think we have made the best plans for our travel through life. But just as on a trip where detours are almost inevitable, so are the events in life that disrupt our best laid plans-or at least the way we wanted things to turn out.

Have you ever noticed that detours come at the most inopportune time? They never come when you have plenty of time. They never come when you're out for a Sunday drive. They always come when you are in a hurry or you are late for something you had planned.

Have you ever noticed that detours are never a better road? When you get taken off the Interstate by a detour, it's never to put you on a better road. It's usually a very narrow, curvy, rough road that slows you and bogs you down.

I remember going out west one time in the bus. We were headed to Seattle, Washington. We were on the interstate making great time when suddenly, we came upon a detour. The detour took us on a small, winding road out in the middle of nowhere that eventually became a dirt road, which quickly made the inside of the bus dusty. We were all coughing and hacking and sneezing. It seemed to take us forever to get back to pavement. We had to stop and thoroughly clean the inside of the bus and wash the outside. We were pulling a trailer that had our equipment in it, so we had to stop and wipe all the equipment down. All of this put us behind our schedule.

Life detours are similar. They don't usually happen at the best times, and they are never convenient. Detours in life almost always involve traveling through a valley.

Sometimes life detours and valleys can contain sickness, divorce, loss of job, or even death. I have discovered that we learn a lot about ourselves in the valleys of life. Not everything we learn about ourselves in the valleys of life is positive.

We may learn some truths about ourselves that are not desirable. We can become aware of discontentment, jealousy, envy, resentment, people we haven't forgiven, or misplaced priorities as we go through disappointments and face circumstances we had not planned.

Truth is, detours in life are never fun. I think mostly because we don't see them coming. Most of the time, they are just around a curve where you can't even brace yourself for them. Isn't it amazing how quickly life can change? Isn't it crazy how you can go from feeling good about your life and your walk with the Lord and then suddenly, BAM!!!....you find yourself facing another detour.

Detours can often bring about fear, anxiety, sadness, loneliness, discouragement, or depression. A psychology instructor had just finished a lecture on mental health and was giving an oral quiz. Speaking specifically about depression, she asked, "How would you diagnose a patient who walks back and forth screaming at the top of his lungs one minute, then sits in a chair weeping uncontrollably the next?" A young man in the back of the class raised his hand and answered, "A basketball coach?"

We laugh but it seems that the detour that David was on brought about those same types of emotions. In Psalm 42, he almost seems like two different people having a conversation with each other. He is talking to himself and then answering himself. David asked himself, "Why am I afraid?"

He answered himself, "You need to have hope in the Lord!" He asked, "Why am I scared?" He answered himself, "Look to God for your help. "

We also find that David went through these same emotions between Psalms 22 and 23. David is so sure and confident in his walk with the Lord in Psalm 23.

"The Lord is my Shepherd," he said. "Yea, though I walk through the valley of the shadow of death, I will fear no evil for Thou are with me."

David seems to be so sure that God is with Him in this passage but in Psalm 22, he felt like God had left him when he said, "My God my God, why have you forsaken me?"

I don't know how far apart these two Psalms were written. It could have been years, months, weeks, or days. But isn't it interesting how detours can affect you emotionally and even affect your relationship with the Lord at times? Is it possible to go through things in life that shake you to the core?

Yes... you are a Christian. Yes... you love the Lord. Yes... you have faith, but can we still experience fear, anxiousness, and loneliness? Yes, Yes, and Yes!

The apostle Paul certainly understood abrupt changes and detours. He had faced just about any kind of setback, disruption, chaos, and detour known to man. But, he had learned to be content in every situation.

The word "content" means pleased and satisfied: not needing more.[1] Paul came to a place in his life (not a physical place but a spiritual place) where he felt divine contentment.

"Not that I was ever in need, for I have learned how to be content with whatever I have. I know how to live on almost nothing or with everything. I have learned the secret of living in every situation, whether it is with a full stomach or empty, with plenty or little."

Philippians 4:11-12 NLT

I think this is what Paul is trying to say, "Great news, I don't have to panic when my circumstances change!" God has made it possible to be content no matter my situation. When I am in my worst situation, I can still look around and see the sweetness of God.

Paul is saying to all believers that we can **enjoy the scenery along the detour!**

Paul shared some great ways we can

enjoy the scenery along the detour. As we go through these verses, soak in the words of Paul and be encouraged.

SECTION 1

I Can Enter His Presence

CHAPTER 1

*"Do not be anxious about anything,
but in every situation, by prayer and
petition, with thanksgiving, present
your requests to God."*

Philippians 4:6 NIV

Do not be anxious about
anything? Yeah right! Was it easy for
Paul to say? Well, not really. If anyone
had the right to be anxious, it was Paul.
If anyone had the right to the nervous

irritation of a gnawing anxiety (which originally means tears the heart apart and makes a man quite incapable of doing the right thing)[2] we all know it was Paul.

Yet it is Paul saying, "Don't worry."

It was Jesus that said, "Take no thought."[3] Take no thought of what you shall eat or drink or wear. Don't even think about it! "Take no thought for the morrow" is even a bigger statement. Each day is going to bring its own trouble. Why should you add to it by worrying about it?

Jesus, the disciples, or the Holy Spirit must have conveyed that message to Paul because that's exactly what he's saying here: <u>don't worry about anything.</u>

To quote my friend, Carol G. Dry (Susan Whisnant's mom):

"If you're gonna pray, don't worry.
If your gonna worry, don't pray."

But, Paul was in prison writing this. More than likely facing a death sentence. Don't worry? Don't be anxious? About anything?

It's difficult for me. I come from a long line of worriers. My momma is a worrier, and her momma was a worrier (not sure about her momma). When my momma doesn't have something to worry about, she worries about it. So....I get it honestly. Telling a worrier not to worry is almost like telling a tall guy not to be tall or a short guy not to be short. It's much easier said than done. This seems so easy for Paul, but I am sure it was a process for him to learn this.

Then Paul says;

- ***"But in Every Situation"*** - this means exactly what it says.

We can carry everything before the Lord. There is nothing which pertains to body, mind, home, friends, conflicts, losses, trials, hopes, fears, or anything else you can reference to which we may not go and spread it all out before the Lord.[4]

He continues;

- ***"By Prayer and Petition"*** *-* I have read many commentaries on this. Many of them differ on this to some degree. I prefer what the Cambridge Bible says on this. Cambridge says that basically Paul is talking about worshipping God and speaking to Him freely and fully.[5] The two words go hand in hand. We should never really ask anything of God without first acknowledging who He is.

I love the quote from A. W. Tozier that says, "God wants worshippers before workers; indeed, the only acceptable workers are those that have learned the lost art of worship."[6]

GOD WANTS WORSHIPPERS BEFORE WORKERS.

When we worship with an obedient heart and an open and repentant spirit, God is glorified, Christians are purified, the church is edified, and the lost are evangelized. These are all the elements of true worship.[7]

He probably won't respond
to your honey-do-list.

Jesus said the same thing when his disciples asked Him to teach them to pray. He said, "Our Father in heaven, hallowed be Your name."[8]
Always start off by recognizing who He is and that He is to be honored.

Paul then includes;

- *"With Thanksgiving"* - which goes with prayer and petition, being thankful for everything He has done for you.

The *Cambridge Bible for Schools and Colleges* says the attitude of the Christian should always be one of thanksgiving and all prayer ought to include the element of thanksgiving for mercies temporal and spiritual.[9]
The privilege of prayer is an abiding theme for grateful praise.

ALL PRAYER OUGHT TO INCLUDE THE ELEMENT OF THANKSGIVING.

Then Paul says,

- *"Present your requests to God"* - This one hit me hard when I started studying this. I am quick to talk to my wife about a need or my friend or my pastor or anyone else besides God. Not only my needs but my complaints as well. Aren't we all a little guilty of that? Don't we sometimes talk to others about needs, concerns, wants, problems, desires, and even other people (which is gossiping) instead of God?

Matthew Poole says, "Our affectionate desires should be opened to God, and poured forth before Him; not that He is ignorant of us or our wants in any circumstances, but that He accounts Himself glorified by our addresses to Him, in seeking to be approved and assisted of Him in every condition."[10]

CHAPTER 2

*"Do not be anxious about anything,
but in every situation, by prayer and
petition, with thanksgiving, present
your requests to God."*

Philippians 4:6 NIV

Just being honest, praying for
long periods of time is difficult for me.
I wished I could tell you that I have the
ability to go into the closet and spend
hours on my knees before God. But, I

don't. I have the attention span of a gnat. After about 4 to 5 minutes (or less) I'm thinking about something else. I think of something I forgot to do yesterday or something Dana told me to do last week that I just now remembered.

War Room? Not hardly, more like WIMP room. That movie really inspired me (for about 2 hours). I am being serious. I have watched it a few times. Now, I am hoping it will just inspire me to clean my closet. Ugh! Seriously though, it is one of my favorite movies, and I do wish I could be like that sweet lady who would go in the closet and pray for long periods of time.

Read my Bible?
Yes.

Listen to sermons?
Sometimes all day....I am serious.

Talk to you about scripture?
My favorite thing.

Personal Worship Time?
Oh yeah, I love listening to songs and worshiping and crying and worshiping and crying but....

Prayer Life?
Epic failure.

Or at least that's the way I feel at times. Let me be very clear about this: when I tell someone that I will pray for them, I do sincerely. I really do! But, can I be accused of going into the woods and spending days or even hours pleading before God? No.

Am I proud of that? No!

I look at my conversations with my wife and guess what? We don't talk for

8 straight hours at a time either. Why? Because we live life together. We are interested in what each other is doing, but we don't have time to just sit and talk for hours. We talk in the morning for a little while; we make short calls (popcorn calls I call them) periodically throughout the day to one another and then we talk mostly at night. But, guess what? Some of our sweetest moments are when we just sit beside each other. Sometimes we hold hands. Sometimes we stare passionately into each other's eyes (mostly joking about this one). But, it's not always talking.

I feel like my relationship with God is the same way to some degree. God and I live life together. Sometimes I think He would just like for me to be quiet (so does my wife) and listen. But then, I read quotes from some great preachers. Some leave me inspired while others leave me embarrassed.

"I have so much to do today that I shall spend the first three hours in prayer."[11]

Martin Luther

"Are you kidding me?"

Eric Bennett

I do like what C. H. Spurgeon said. He said, "True prayer is measured by weight, not by length. A single groan before God may have more fullness of prayer in it than a fine oration of great length."[12]

At least this gives me some hope!

"Talking to men for God is a great thing, but talking to God for men is greater still."[13]

E.M. Bounds

Maybe we should all learn from the one who knew the most about prayer: Jesus. He seemed to have an incredible prayer life.

Jesus prayed? The book of Mark pictures Jesus getting up very early in the morning, while it was still dark, and going to pray.

"Now in the morning, having risen a long while before daylight, He went out and departed to a solitary place; and there He prayed."

Mark 1:35 NKJV

Ever wonder why Jesus went to pray?

1. To get His next move?
2. To re-energize?
3. Could it be simply because **He loved His dad?**

Jesus talked to His Father quite a bit. Jesus obviously knew the importance of constant communication with His Father. It also must have been an incredible sight to watch and listen to Jesus talk to His Father. The disciples came to Jesus after He was finished praying. They dare not interrupt Him.

"Now it came to pass, as He was praying in a certain place, when He ceased, that one of His disciples said to Him, 'Lord, teach us to pray, as John also taught his disciples.'"

Luke 11:1 NKJV

The disciples never asked Jesus to teach them how to walk on water. They never asked Him to teach them how to feed thousands with only a little boys lunch. They never asked Him to teach them to raise the dead. They asked Him to teach them to pray.

Jesus obviously loved talking to His Father. He wanted that closeness that can only come from spending quality time with Him.

I often call my kids on the phone just to see how their day went. I just want to hear their voices. I love it even more when they call me. It literally makes my day. Don't you think God is the same way when it comes to hearing from one of His kids? I do!

Our attic in our house looks like a tornado came through and ransacked the whole thing. It's scary. It has one little pig like trail through it from one end to the other, and everything that we ever need out of it always seems to be on the opposite end of the entrance. What is it full of? Everything our kids have done since they were little. Every picture of them since birth. Every picture they've colored, every test they've taken, and every trophy or ribbon they've ever won. All the cards and notes they've ever written to us. There are science projects from years ago. Hmmm.... that could explain the smell!

Basically, everything that has anything to do with our kids, that's not in the house somewhere on a wall or table, is in our attic. Why? Because while it may not seem like anything big to you, it's all a treasure to us. They're our kids. We adore them. Everything they've ever done is incredible to us. It's looking as though we will never get rid of any of it. We will keep it till the end of our time. We may go up at some point and rearrange (if we become brave enough) but we will never throw any of it away. It's important to us.

Did you know that God keeps your prayers? Revelation 5:8 says He has them all in a golden bowl. Why? Because they are important to Him. He keeps our conversations that we have with Him. He keeps our petitions we make to Him. He refers to our prayers as fragrant incense: sweet smelling to Him.

Your grandmother's prayers she prayed for you that you didn't even know about are in a golden bowl. Your prayers that you have prayed for your son or daughter that God would save them are in a golden bowl. All the prayers that you've prayed for your husband or wife are in a golden bowl.

The prayers you've prayed for the sick, hurting, or lost are in a golden bowl. All the prayers of the Saints are kept by God. He adores you. He loves you. He wants to hear from you. How about filling up a golden bowl with prayers by talking to the One that wants to hear from you the most?

What a friend we have in Jesus
All our sins and griefs to bear
What a privilege to carry
Everything to God in prayer
Oh, what peace we often forfeit
Oh, what needless pain we bear
All because we do not carry
Everything to God in prayer[14]

This is one of my favorite old hymns that reminds us that we should take everything to God in Prayer. *Here's the greatest reality of it all:*

PRAYER CHANGES THINGS!

You know what my prayers change most of the time?

ME!

You have the great privilege to enter His presence and talk to God about your problems! And, **enjoy the scenery along the detour!**

My daughter, Erin, taught me a huge lesson on prayer when she was only 16 years old.

Both of my kids taught me as much as I ever taught them.

She had just gotten her license so Dana and I were ready for her to get out and get a job to earn her some gas money. We would occasionally mention it to her. We were trying to be nice and inconspicuous. She would always say, "I'm praying about it."

Erin prayed about everything in her life.

One day I came in, saw her sitting on the couch, and so I became a little frustrated. I said, "Erin, don't you think it's time to get out and find a job? Have you put any applications in anywhere? Have you been to any businesses or talked to anybody about a job?" She said, "I'm still praying about it." This aggravated me to no end. I became down right mad. I wanted her to put legs on her prayers. I said, "Erin, do you really expect someone to come to our front door and ask you to work for them?" She just looked at her dad like he was a big ole dummy. Guess what?

He was a big dummy! I kid you not; I bet it wasn't two hours later that our neighbor, Larry Stinson, rang our door bell, and said, "Hey Eric, do you think Erin might want a job working in the jewelry store with Melinda and me?"

I'm not sure that Larry picked up on the blank stare and the fact that my jaw hit the floor. I just simply replied, "Yes, yes, I guess she would like a job Larry."

Erin worked with Larry and Melinda at the jewelry store all the way through high school and most of college.

Big lesson learned by me;
Prayer really does change things!

If life throws you a detour and you're forced to take an alternative route, the scenery is so much better when we talk to Him along the way!

CHAPTER 3

"Do not be anxious about anything, but in every situation, by prayer and petition, with thanksgiving, present your requests to God."

Philippians 4:6 NIV

Worshipping the Lord and coming before Him with thankfulness as we pray are two keys to getting our prayers answered. On a personal note, I have so much to be thankful for. Don't you? I could thank Him and worship Him from now through eternity, and it wouldn't be sufficient for what He has done for me.

We can all find things in our life to be thankful for and reasons to worship Him. If you are having a bad day or a day where you are having a hard time remembering what God has done for you, just look to Calvary. Just think about the grace that was poured over you there!

"For by grace are ye saved through faith; and that not of yourselves: it is the gift of God: Not of works, lest any man should boast."

Ephesians 2:8-9 KJV

What exactly is grace?

"Grace is God's unmerited love."[15]

Adrian Rodgers

*"Grace is the empowering presence
of God enabling you to be who
He created you to be, and to do what
He has called you to do."*[16]

James Ryle

**"Grace is the sole basis for both new life
and spiritual vitality."**

Stanley Grants

These really say more about what Grace does than what it is. Grace in the Greek is Charis.[17]

The C is silent so it's pronounced Ha-rees, and at its core, grace is the unmerited, undeserved, unearned kindness and favor of God.

GRACE IS THE UNMERITED, UNDESERVED, UNEARNED KINDNESS AND FAVOR OF GOD.

Here is a little story of how I was shown grace in my life by my dad. Dana and I were married December 7, 1985 on her 17th birthday. She was too young to know any better! We were high school sweet hearts and had been dating since she was 14 years old. We had a wedding date set for August 10th when she was only 16 years old, but I was too nervous about it so we put it off for 5 months till she could grow up some!

At the same time, I had a full ride scholarship to college to sing in the Wallace State Community College singers. I am very thankful for my upbringing. However, mom and dad couldn't pay for college. Although we had most of what we needed, the family paying for my college was not going to be a possibility. It was going to be tough financially even with a full ride. A Scholarship was my only hope.

Hmmm…what to do? Go to college or get a job and not let this girl get away? She came from good stock (meaning her mom was beautiful too). I could not let her get away. So, I prayed about it for about 2 seconds (I recommend longer). I started fasting after breakfast one morning and fasted all the way up until lunch (I recommend longer). I wanted to marry her so badly so I asked her. She said.....YES!!!

Her mom and dad had to sign for her to get married. What were they thinking? For some reason, they liked me. I had them fooled! On the rehearsal night of our wedding, I had just gotten paid and I really wanted this event to be special in every way for Dana. So, I decided to go buy her a new necklace. I wanted to surprise her with something that night just make it extra special. I had to drive a good piece out of my way to pick the necklace up. When I was leaving the jewelry store, my old jalopy of a truck wouldn't start. The battery was dead. It took what seemed like an eternity to find someone with jumper cables to get me going. I finally got to the rehearsal dinner about 30 minutes late only to find Dana crying uncontrollably. I asked her what was wrong. She said, "I thought you had run away." I had never heard of a run-away groom, but I am sure they exist. I was not one of them. I was crazy about this girl.

I'm still crazy about her by the way.

Our wedding day was here. I could describe how incredible Dana looked on our wedding day but that would fill up a whole different book by itself. We had a beautiful, small wedding and we were off to our honeymoon. Dana was wearing a gray skirt with a pink top. She looked amazing!

I have already said that I wanted this night to be special but I didn't do a good job on planning ahead. In all the movies I had watched that had romantic scenes, the couple was usually drinking a glass of wine. So, the first stop I wanted to make was to the liquor store. Neither one of us drank or had ever been in a liquor store but again, I wanted this night to be perfect, so a nice bottle of wine was a must. As soon as we left the reception, we drove to Decatur, Alabama. I used to work close to Decatur and had passed by a liquor store on my way to work many times. It had a big, neon sign blinking. This was the ideal place to get what I needed. As we pulled in, I was getting more and more nervous by the second and so was Dana. Was anyone going to see us? Was anyone going to recognize that I sang gospel music? I got out of the car, looked around to see if I knew anyone that I went to church with (joking), and hurried in. I had no idea what I was looking for other than a bottle of wine. I didn't want to ask anyone for help, so I just grabbed the first thing I came to that said "WINE." I scurried up to the counter with my head down, paid for it, and darted out the door. I had purchased my first bottle of wine for only 3 dollars and it was going to be good. Everything was now perfect. We were about to be on our way to an exciting evening (not here to debate drinking, we will do that in person next time we see each other).

But....my car wouldn't start. Yep! This was the second evening in a row that one of my two old dilapidated vehicles wouldn't crank. But this time, it was in the parking lot of a liquor store with a neon sign blinking saying, "Here we are! Here we are!" Well, that was what it was saying in my mind! I was devastated. I was totally embarrassed.

I just knew God was punishing me for this. I had bought the wine and God was angry at me so he sabotaged my car. Oh, the guilt I felt. I jumped out of the car, grabbed the bottle of wine, threw it up against the wall to shatter it, only to have it bounce back and hit me. Again, let me remind you, it only cost 3 bucks. The bottle was plastic. What made all of this even worse was that my brand-new bride was sitting in the car watching this whole thing go down. Her new husband had already gone mad. Now I was even more embarrassed.

Who could I call? Who could I call that could fix my car that wouldn't rake me over the coals for being at the liquor store? Who could I call that wouldn't judge me?

I called my dad. Yep, Deacon Carl H. Bennett. Yes, I said deacon. My dad had been a deacon for many years. He was a good man but very stern. He didn't put up with much of anything, especially drinking. He had showed mercy on me several other times before for different things but he wouldn't this time, not for drinking. I thought I was nervous when I pulled into this store but now I was terrified. I fully expected to get a chewing out at the least and possibly punched in the face (not really but he probably should have). My dad showed up with my brother,

Perry.

How was my dad gonna respond?

Not only did he not say anything about where the car was located (knowing I was ashamed of myself already) he put his arms around me and hugged me. Yes, he hugged me. And he just held on. I was in tears and knowing I was feeling guilty over my actions, He didn't condemn me. He just hugged me.

WHAT GRACE MY DAD HAD SHOWN!

My dad also brought us his truck to drive and told me to have fun and he would handle everything with repairing my car. I wish I could tell my dad thanks one more time.

I am reminded of the loving father in Luke 15:11-32. You know the story well I am sure. Most people have titled this passage the parable of the prodigal son or the parable of the two prodigal sons but I had much rather call it the story of the loving father.

The father had two sons. The younger son had taken his share of the of his inheritance. The older son would get two thirds and the rest would be divided between the other sons. In going to collect his inherence, the younger son was basically saying to his dad that I wished you were dead.

In those days, a father could either grant the inheritance before or after his death, but it was usually done *after*. The younger son asks for a special exception. The father clearly illustrates God's love. His love would allow rebellion and would respect man's will. The father more than knew what would happen to the son, but allowed him to go his course none the less.[18]

After blowing all his possessions and coming to his lowest of lows eating with the pigs he was hired to feed, the son decides to go home to hopefully just become one of his father's hired servants. The son already had in his mind what he was going to say to his father. I am sure he rehearsed his speech all the way home.

His father had obviously been hoping for him to come home every day. He saw the young boy coming down the road while he was still a good way off. The father ran to his son, had compassion on him, kissed him, and held him. Yep, I said he just held him.

WHAT GRACE THIS
FATHER HAD SHOWN!

The son tried his best to give his speech to his dad but his dad would have none of it. Right in the middle of the son telling the father how unworthy he was to be his son, the father told his servants to start the feast. His boy was home. The father put his best robe on the boy's back, a ring on his finger, and sandals on his feet. All of this was a sign of restoration.

When a Christian dies, saying that "God needs another angel" or "Another angel went home to heaven" is actually an insult to the person even though you may mean well. When you come to the Lord, He

won't even accept you as a hired servant
or an angel. You are immediately a son or
daughter. It was party time. The wayward
boy had come home.

---

*WHEN YOU COME TO THE LORD,
HE WON'T EVEN ACCEPT YOU AS A
HIRED SERVANT OR AN ANGEL.*

THINGS TO PONDER

1. The Prodigal son was in the pig
    pen probably talking to the pigs. I
    wonder what kind of advice the pigs
    were giving him. This brings me
    to this question: what pigs are you
    getting your advice from? Anything
    you're putting in your mind except
    advice from a Christian counselor or
    Christian material is from the world
    (pigs).

*"Blessed is the man Who walks not in
the counsel of the ungodly, Nor stands
in the path of sinners, Nor sits in the seat
of the scornful; But his delight is in the
law of the LORD, And in His law he
meditates day and night."*

Psalms 1:1-2 NKJV

2. The Prodigal son lived with the well (his Father), but he chose to leave with only a bucket of water. He lived at home where he had access to everything his father had but chose to leave with only a small portion.

"For every beast of the forest is Mine, And the cattle on a thousand hills."

Psalms 50:10 NKJV

Oh, and by the way, He owns the hills too! Let's face it; He owns it all! Why in the world would we settle for a bucket of water when we could know and live in the fellowship of the Living Water, the Eternal Well, the Everlasting Fountain?

3. Did you know that when a wayward child chooses to come home that the Father in Heaven always rejoices?

Luke 15:10 says that there is rejoicing in the presence of the angels of God over one sinner who repents. Most preachers say that the angels are rejoicing but that's not what the verse says. It's the Father rejoicing in the presence of angels over someone that's come home.

4. If you are not spiritually where you should be, God will receive you if you come to Him with a repentant heart. No matter what you have done, He loves you and wants you to come home.

"For God so Loved the world that He gave His only begotten Son that whosoever believes in Him should not perish but have everlasting life."

John 3:16

WHAT GRACE THE HEAVENLY FATHER SHOWS!

Grace is God's way of making it possible for you and me to have an incredible relationship with the Heavenly Father.

It's by grace and grace alone that we can enter His presence.

Only by entering His presence can we enjoy the scenery along the detour.

SECTION 2

I Can Enjoy His Peace

CHAPTER 4

"And the peace of God, which transcends all understanding, will guard your hearts and your minds in Christ Jesus."

Philippians 4:7 NIV

There is a reason this verse starts off with a conjunction. It is because it is so closely tied to the preceding verse. The biggest reason that we will experience such an overwhelming and unexplainable peace of God in our lives is because we've done what verse six says to do.

1. We have worshipped the Lord.

2. We have talked to the Lord about everything.

3. We have thanked the Lord.

> *"You, Lord, give perfect peace to those who keep their purpose firm and put their trust in you."*

> *Isaiah 26:3 GNT*

The peace of God is promised to those that stay focused on the Lord. I have noticed in my personal life that the bigger I see God, the smaller my problems seem. The more I look to Him, focus on Him, and keep my mind on Him, I have a harder time seeing my troubles. More of Him, less of them!

- *"Which Transcends All Understanding"-* most likely means "beyond all human comprehension." Maybe Paul meant that God's peace totally transcends the merely human, unbelieving mind which is full of anxiety because it's full of doubt and can't think higher than itself.[19] But, I tend to believe that Paul is saying that the peace God gives cannot be understood by man. The only way a person could begin to comprehend it, is by experiencing it.

THE PEACE OF GOD CANNOT BE EXPLAINED, BUT IT CAN BE EXPERIENCED.

Earlier I said this book was inspired by the late great Randy Wright. Randy had a ton of friends. I was glad to just know him. The church he pastored is just a small country church in Guin, Alabama. Most people never got the opportunity to meet Randy or go to his church but I am thankful God let our paths cross.

As I sat across from Randy in his office that day and listened to his telling about the grim circumstances he was facing, I was looking into the eyes of someone that had a peace I didn't understand. He had this peace!

"The peace of God will guard your hearts and your minds in Christ Jesus."

Paul probably had a guard guarding him at the very moment he was writing this. The guard was more than likely walking back and forth in front of the door with a big spear in his hand, not letting anyone come in without permission. This possibly put the thought of the guard in Paul's mind.

Proverbs 4:23 tells us to guard our hearts. When Solomon tells us to guard our heart, he's referring to the inner core of a person, the thoughts, feelings, desires, will, and the choices that make that person who he or she is.[20]

Proverbs 23:7 tells us our thoughts most often dictate who we become. Solomon is saying that the mind of a man reflects who he really is, not simply his actions or words. You can't really know a man by only watching or listening to him. Motives for actions are often deceitful and words often empty.

Paul reminds us that if we are going

to receive the peace of God, it's a matter of the mind.

"Finally, believers, whatever is true, whatever is honorable and worthy of respect, whatever is right and confirmed by God's word, whatever is pure and wholesome, whatever is lovely and brings peace, whatever is admirable and of good repute; if there is any excellence, if there is anything worthy of praise, think continually on these things [center your mind on them, and implant them in your heart]. The things which you have learned and received and heard and seen in me, practice these things [in daily life], and the God [who is the source] of peace and well-being will be with you."

Philippians 4:8-9 AMP

Sometimes our minds become cloudy with

negativity or doubt. We must re-mind ourselves. When I say *re*-mind, I mean this: "re" is a prefix meaning "again, or again and again."[21]

Mind means "the element, part, substance, or process that reasons, thinks, feels, wills, perceives, judges, etc."[22]

You are putting on a new person every day. It's an "again and again" transformation. We have to *re*-mind every day. When we pray, we are *re*-minding ourselves that God is cap-able. When we pray, we are *re*-minding ourselves that God is caring. When we pray, we are *re*-minding ourselves of how all-knowing God is.

He is Alpha and Omega. He sees the end from the beginning. He already knows our outcome.

PRAYER RE-MINDS US.

The key is that we are *re*-minded. No matter what our minds say, if we will pray like the previous verse says to do, we can be *re*-minded.

"Do not be conformed to this world but be transformed by the renewing of your mind."

Romans 12:2

Paul is reminding us to that it takes a conscience effort to be transformed. We must make up our minds daily.

CHAPTER 5

"And the peace of God, which transcends all understanding, will guard your hearts and your minds in Christ Jesus."

Philippians 4:7 NIV

Peace is defined several ways. One is the state of tranquility or serenity. Also, the freedom of the mind from annoyance, distraction, anxiety, etc.[23]

As I was studying on peace, statistics on anxiety disorders kept showing up. I was shocked at the percentage of people that deal with this according to studies.

Anxiety disorders affect millions of adults every year. Some statistics say that possibly up to 30% of all adults deal with them. Some don't seek help or they are just misdiagnosed. Over 42 Billion dollars are spent on anxiety disorders every year. Almost one third of all mental health funds spent every year is on anxiety issues.[24]

As I was reading and thinking on these statistics, I am reminded of my own personal experience. Although small to some and not nearly as in depth as most people's problems with anxiety, I thought I would include my struggles. Ever since I have been singing, I have had a nervous problem that I haven't been able to overcome. When I first started singing full time 25 years ago, it really became noticeable not only to me but to the others I was singing with. My nervousness manifested itself with a swallowing problem every time I took a lead on a song. I went to 3 or 4 different ENTs (ear, nose and throat specialists) with no results. I really didn't know what the problem was and I was trying everything to get rid of it. I even went to a psychologist because I thought it might just be in my mind.

Let me include this: I prayed over my situation. I fasted over my situation. I cried over it. Dana and I prayed over it together. I confessed all my sins that I had ever committed and some I hadn't. I tried everything. I shared with close preacher friends and was prayed over many times. I memorized bible verses including 2 Timothy 1:7 that says God hath not given us a spirit of fear, but of power, love and a sound mind. I quoted it along with many others over and over and over before I would go out and sing. Nothing worked. It seemed as though God said, "This is something you are going to have to deal with."

GOD HATH NOT GIVEN US A SPIRIT OF FEAR, BUT OF POWER, LOVE, AND A SOUND MIND.

I used to think if I could get close enough to God that He would relieve and heal me of all my problems. He didn't want me to suffer. But, then I read 2 Corinthians 12:8-10:

"Three different times I begged the Lord to take it away, and each time He said, 'My grace is all you need. My power works best in weakness.' So now I am glad to boast about my weaknesses, so that the power of

Christ can work through me. That's why I take pleasure in my weaknesses, and in the insults, hardships, persecutions, and troubles that I suffer for Christ. For when I am weak, then I am strong."

2 Corinthians 12:8-10 NLT

This is Paul saying that he had a thorn in the flesh that God would not remove even after much prayer. This gave me a peace about my situation. Just a side note: there is an answer in the Bible to every difficulty we may face.

THERE IS AN ANSWER IN THE BIBLE TO EVERY DIFFICULTY WE MAY FACE.

I did finally find an incredible ENT

that diagnosed me with the right condition: Nerves! I don't even know if there is a medical term for this. He said he had seen plenty of people with this difficulty though. He prescribed something that will take the edge off the nervous problems. I still use it over 20 years later, especially in big concerts.

I am, however, still reminded by my nerves every time I get up to sing that I can do nothing by myself. I am nothing in and of myself. I need God to show up and show out (in me personally) every time I get up on stage to sing or preach.

If you are on some type of prescription for medical anxiety problems, don't think you are by yourself. Don't think you are weird. Don't think you are unfit to serve the Lord. Paul had problems he couldn't overcome that seemed to drive him crazy and that the Lord wouldn't remove, yet he had the peace of God. We can enjoy the peace of God in our lives even through our own issues.

I pray that you find the peace of God in your life. I know you are probably going through something even as you are reading this. Remember that while you are praying for God to calm your situation or circumstances, He may be looking to just calm you.

---

*OFTEN, WE WANT GOD TO
CALM THE STORM
WHEN HE MAY CHOOSE TO CALM US
IN THE MIDST OF THE STORM.*

This sweet peace of God allows us to enjoy the scenery along the detour.

SECTION 3

I Can Experience His Power

CHAPTER 6

*"I can do all things through Christ
who strengthens me."*

Philippians 4:13 NKJV

What a great truth this is!!!

Lots of people have used this verse to help them think more positive thoughts or dream bigger dreams. But, when kept in context, it means something totally different. I just want to remind you that this is one of the Pauline epistles that was written from what could have been a small, dark, and stank jail cell. It was written not when Paul was on top of the world, living out one of his many dreams or wanting his thinking to become more positive. It was written in one of Paul's dark times in his life.

Paul had just penned in the previous verse that he had learned to be content no matter his situation, circumstances or his detours. He's not saying that we can always conquer the world but that we have Someone we can draw strength from when the world conquers us.[25]

Paul knew he had a specific purpose given him by God. But the road to fulfilling that purpose would often be filled with potholes and Detours. **Paul knew what he would draw from to get him to his**

destination would not be inner strength but strength found only in the person of the Holy Spirit.

God has a purpose for every one of us. He, with that purpose, gives us the Holy Spirit to make sure that we can live out that purpose.

The enemy would like nothing more than to weigh us down with circumstances, problems, and cares of this world. But, God has promised us that we are overcomers. Not in and of ourselves of course, but through the strength He gives. Thank God for the Helper!

"The Helper, the Holy Spirit, whom the Father will send in my name, will teach you everything and make you remember all that I have told you."

John 14:26 GNT

Jesus likened the Holy Spirit to a well of living water, which He said would spring up within us and lead us to eternal life. Like water to a parched ground, the Holy Spirit offers refreshment and help to our weary souls.

What is your need today?

Is it for companionship?
The Holy Spirit is with you. A Friend that sticks closer than a brother.

Is it for comfort?
The Holy Spirit stands ready to help. He is an ever-present help in the time of need.

Is it for an advocate?
He is ready to plead your case.

Erwin Lutzer writes in his article, "The Holy Spirit, Our Helper," that although we are in dwelt by the Holy Spirit, not all believers are filled with the Spirit. To be filled with the Spirit means that we are experiencing the Holy Spirit's gentle guidance and control in our lives. To be filled with the Spirit means that the Spirit is reproducing His fruit within us. We should never think that the filling of the Spirit is just for those Christians who are the spiritually elite. The Spirit is not for those who "have it all together" but to the rest of us so that we might be able to "get it all together." The filling of the Spirit is for the most discouraged, failing Christian, but in order for us to enjoy the Spirit's ministry, we must meet some basic conditions.[26]

Living a faith filled life is one of those conditions. Hebrews 11:6 says "But without

Faith it is impossible to please Him."

Another condition is living a consistent life of confession. My favorite Bible verse is 1 John 1:9 "If we confess our sins, He is faithful to forgive us our sins and cleanse us from all unrighteousness." But, when we willingly have unconfessed sin in our life, we grieve the Holy Spirit. He knows the damage that sin does in our lives. When He is grieved, His ministry within us is quenched.

REMEMBER, YOUR BODY IS THE TEMPLE OF THE HOLY SPIRIT. IT'S WHERE HE LIVES!

To truly draw from and experience the goodness of God's gift of the Holy Spirit, we must strive to live a life that would please Him. His constant filling is something we must long for. DL Moody was once asked why he had to be filled with the Spirit so often and he simply said, "Because I leak."

Several times in scripture Paul refers to our conduct. He says in Philippians 1:27, "Let your conduct be worthy of the gospel of Christ." We all seem to have that one sin that sometimes hinders us or slows us down from being all God intended us to be or becoming what He wants us to become. It's that one thing that can hinder us from His purpose being fulfilled in our life.

Reminds me of a story of my son, Zac. He is as close to perfect as any kid I've ever been around. He has always had a conscience that was bigger than he was. After he committed to Christ it was even bigger! We could tell at a very young age that the Lord had something very special in store for Zac. He could play the guitar at a very young age and could musically hear different parts way before his teen years. His only fault was, and I do mean his only fault, was he had no concept of time. He didn't live in any time zone. Time just didn't register. We knew he would be late to his own funeral!

We thought it would get better with age but, unfortunately, it didn't. His high school years was often a struggle getting him out of bed to get to school on time. Here's the thing, his grades were perfect, I mean straight A's. He was very active in church. Just an incredibly respectful kid, but always late.

Surely it will get better in college? Nope! If anything, it got worse. Of course, we became a little more lenient on him because he was a big college student now. But, he was still dreadfully late to class. Sometimes, he would have buddies come over and they would stay up late in the night or early in the morning playing video games or watching TV. Then, he would want to sleep all day. But, his grades were still great. Ugh! We really struggled with getting on to him because he was perfect in every other way. He wasn't out drinking, or partying or carousing around. He was at home, but.....sleeping!

I came in from town one day and jumped on the lawnmower to mow the yard. It was probably 1pm. I noticed his car in the driveway so I jumped off lawnmower, ran upstairs, and there he was, still in the bed. I woke him up and said, "Zac, I thought you had school today".

"I do. What time is it?"

I said, "It's 1pm. What time is your class?"

He said, "It started at noon".

I got so angry I could have bit a nail in two. He must be disciplined. He would have to walk where ever he went or ride a bike. I said, "Give me your car keys. I'm not putting up with this anymore! As long as you're under this roof....blah blah blah!" And then, I walked out!

Later that evening when Dana got home she asked where Zac was. I didn't know. He wasn't at home. She called him. He was at work. He worked at the church…five miles from home.

But, how did he get there? How did he get his guitar there? How did he get all his gear there and the huge backpack?

He rode his bicycle. Yep! **FIVE** miles on a main highway!

Guess who got a greater chewing that evening by his wife for making her baby ride a bike with a boat load of stuff on his back for FIVE Miles on a main road?
ME!

Guess who got to drive his truck to church to pick his son and his bike up?
ME!

Guess who is scared of his 115lb wife?
ME!

Guess who was on time for work and school from that point on though?
ZAC!

Guess who is working as a Worship Pastor and is always on time now?

ZAC!

*Guess who still looks back on that incident
until this day and laughs?
You guessed it: Me, Dana, and Zac*

Zac almost let that one little thing keep him from fulfilling God's purpose in his life. I'm so proud of my little boy! Ok, ok, I'm so proud of my full-grown son (that will always be my little boy).

"Therefore, since we are surrounded by such a huge crowd of witnesses to the life of faith, let us strip off every weight that slows us down, especially the sin that so easily trips us up. And let us run with endurance the race God has set before us."

Hebrews 12:1 NLT

What is the sin that trips you up?

Are you allowing it to keep you from
God's purpose in your life?

There are some things that weigh us down, but there are other things that trip us up. The deadliest threat to faith is sin. Sin in your life keeps you from believing God. If you are going to run the race of faith, you must get rid of the things that weigh you down and the things that cause you to fall. Look into your heart. Is there something you wrestle with again and again? Lay it aside and fully surrender to God!

"If you are having difficulty with faith, try repentance."[27]

Dr. Adrian Rogers

Let me encourage you right now. Lay this book down, repent of anything that may be standing in the way of the Holy Spirit having full access in your life and commit yourself to running the race God has set before you with endurance.

CHAPTER 7

*"I can do all things through Christ
who strengthens me."*

Philippians 4:13 NKJV

It is the Holy Spirit that helps us and gives us the power to look at our problems and face them with the attitude that God's got this! It is the Holy Spirit that helps us to live a life pleasing to God in the face of adversities.

"But ye shall receive power, after that the Holy Ghost is come upon you: and ye shall be witnesses unto me both in Jerusalem, and in all Judaea, and in Samaria, and unto the uttermost part of the earth."

Acts 1:8 KJV

Jesus says that the Holy Spirit will give us power to share the gospel everywhere we go. I think this includes the fact that the Holy Spirit will help us live in such a way, that no matter the circumstances we are facing, people will see how we respond to those circumstances and want what we have.

A great Christian friend of mine told me a story about the time he spent in the army. He had very few friends in the army because of his strong convictions that he lived by. He said, "I always tried to live for Christ everyday no matter what was going on around me." The day he was getting out of the army, two of his fellow soldiers stopped him on the way out and said, "We haven't heard you say one dirty or disrespectful word since you've been in here. We want you to know that the Christian life you lived before us has impacted, influenced and impressed us. Thank you."

"Imitate God, therefore, in everything you do, because you are his dear children. Live a life filled with love, following the example of Christ. He loved us and offered himself as a sacrifice for us, a pleasing aroma to God."

It's only in, by, through, and with the Holy Spirit that we can imitate a true Christ life.

You never know who is watching.

The Holy Spirit will give you the strength and power to share the gospel without using words. The Holy Spirit will also lead you in every circumstance, situation, and detour that you face.

HOLY SPIRIT WILL GIVE YOU STRENGTH AND POWER TO SHARE THE GOSPEL WITHOUT USING WORDS.

I am a grandparent now. My wife and I now live in Grandparentville. I absolutely love it and highly recommend it. It's the greatest season of life for us so far. We get the opportunity to go visit the little princesses once or twice a month. What a treat! As I was going through some of their books expanding my horizon, I noticed a particular book. If I've ever seen the book, I don't remember it but I do remember the rhyme. It has to do with someone called Humpty Dumpty. Anyone remember this? Say it:

Humpty Dumpty sat on a wall,
Humpty Dumpty had a great fall,
All the Kings horses and all the Kings men
Couldn't put Humpty Dumpty together again

My son-in-law, Anthony, is a student pastor and in one of his sermons, he included an illustration about this story. Indulge me for about 3 mins. Humpty Dumpty has some issues. Could we agree on this?

1. He was an egg like guy with arms and legs. He was a freak like character and really weird looking.

2. His mom and dad named him Humpty Dumpty. What happened to Jim, Fred, Tom, and George?

3. Social skills were obviously lacking. He sat on a wall and it looks like he's all alone.

Had a great fall? I don't think so! I believe the dude jumped! It can never be proven, but I believe he did. He had some serious issues. He had fallen apart and here he is trying to get horses and men to put him back together again.

Just like this children's story, there are a lot of folks who feel as if they have fallen apart. Maybe your marriage has fallen apart or your body physically is falling apart. Your wealth or retirement is falling apart and you are uncertain about your financial future. Maybe your kids have gone wayward or they didn't turn out the way you had hoped they would after the way you raised them. God is in the business of fixing things. He loves the broken ones. He loves to shine the brightest when our circumstances seem the darkest.

My daughter was expecting our first grand baby. Dana and I had already decided we were gonna be the best grandparents ever, Super Grands!!!! We got the phone call around 4:30 in the morning. She was going into labor. Although we lived four hours from them, we were not going to be late for this life-changing event. We had already packed our bags when she told us she was pregnant seven months ago so we were ready! We brushed our teeth and jumped in the car. I drove like a mad man to get to Charlotte in time. We made it. We had hoped and had prayed for an easy delivery.

Everything went smooth for the birth part. Avery came and was the most beautiful little girl we had ever seen (looked exactly like her mother). She had a head full of dark hair and was healthy as she could be. But.....then the panic set in.

The doctor couldn't get Erin's bleeding stopped. Anthony was on one side of the bed, Dana was holding little Avery, and I was in the hallway outside the door. I began to see nurses running in and out. Dana came to the door and told me what was going on. They had also called for other doctors to come in and help. It seemed everyone was in a complete frenzy. We were all praying. Erin was praying out loud but with an amazing calmness about her.

Finally, after losing about five pints of blood and seconds before going into emergency surgery, the specialist they had called to come in, looked up at my daughter and said, "the bleeding has stopped." Erin began to thank the doctor. Then, the doctor said something that I will never forget as long as I live. He said, "Erin, I had nothing to do with it. It was the One you were praying to that did this and only Him."

Do you understand?
The doctor didn't know what to
do in this particular circumstance!
He had no way of stopping the bleeding.
God intervened. God showed up.
God changed the situation.

The power of God is available. Some things can only be explained by divine intervention.

When was the last time you've prayed for over ten minutes at a time?

When was the last time you've fasted for something that you can't seem to fix yourself?

The power of God is available for those that have surrendered their life to Christ. Ask God daily for Power to live over your circumstances. He may not lead you around them but He will give you Strength to face them.

It's the power of God that helps us enjoy the scenery along the detour.

SECTION 4

I Can Expect His Provision

CHAPTER 8

*"And my God shall supply all
your needs according to His riches
in glory by Christ Jesus."*

Philippians 4:19 NKJV

Paul had been the recipient of
that which had been brought to him
in the previous verse. He referred to
the offering that had been brought to
him from the Philippian Church, as a
sweet-smelling aroma, an acceptable

sacrifice, well pleasing to God.

And so, he continues with this conjunction with a promise that since they pleased the Lord with their giving that the Lord would supply their needs.

- *"My God"*- Paul uses this very personal term to describe who would be supplying their needs. Paul knew HIS GOD very well and knew that He was capable and willing to take care of their needs like He had his own.

GOD IS CAPABLE AND WILLING TO TAKE CARE OF YOUR NEEDS!

- *"Shall Supply All Your Needs"*-

"I have not seen the righteous forsaken, nor his descendants begging bread."

Psalms 37:25

Paul had more than likely seen this time and time again. How when people gave it would be returned in abundance to them. He knew what Malachi had promised. Paul knew that if they paid their tithes and give offering above and beyond that God would meet their need.

Here's a thought on tithing: since Dana and I have been tithing we have been more blessed than ever in every way. Malachi 3 says to test the Lord. The only place in the Bible where it says we can test Him. He said He would open up the windows of Heaven and pour out on you blessings you wouldn't be able to contain. He also said that He would rebuke the devourer for your sake. In other words, He will protect you. I firmly believe that if you will tithe, God will take care of your every need. Why don't you put Him to the test?

I believe in tithing and giving offerings above and beyond your tithe. I believe that if you will do this, God will make Psalms 37:4-5 come to pass in your life.

"Take delight in the LORD, and he will give you your heart's desires. Commit everything you do to the LORD. Trust him, and he will help you."

Dana and I constantly prayed for our kids when they were little. We prayed that God would use them to honor Him.

Our first hint that God was answering our prayers with Zac was also one of my most embarrassing moments in life.

Zac is a very accomplished musician. He serves now as a worship pastor in a large church for their contemporary service. When he was around thirteen years old, Dana and I started making him take guitar lessons. Yes, I said making him. Oh yeah, he would complain and whine about having to practice. He would also moan about how his fingers hurt from having to push down on the strings on the guitar. But, we still made him practice over and over and over.

One day, Dana and I heard some music playing upstairs. As we listened closely, we noticed that it was Zac playing his guitar. I asked her, did you make him practice? She said, "No, did you make him practice?" All of a sudden, we noticed that we weren't having to make him practice, we couldn't get him to put the guitar down. Seriously, he was carrying it everywhere, playing, and singing for everyone. We would be trying to watch TV and there he would be on the couch playing and singing to the top of his lungs. What have we done? We've created a musical monster!

Seriously though, Dana and I are so proud of him. We couldn't ask for a better son. God truly blessed us with a boy that has become an amazing man of God. When Zac was sixteen, he was asked by a southern gospel artist, Angelina McKeithen, to fill in and sing with her for a few weekends in the summer. This was the answer to our prayers. This was God giving us the desires of our heart. This was the big moment that would launch his career, and if he was going to be close, his parents must be there too. So, we packed a few things in a suitcase (well, I packed a few things, Dana packed for a month) and followed them around for a few of their concerts.

One Sunday afternoon, we were in a church in Georgia. Dana and I walked in and noticed that there was a place right up front for us to sit so we hurried up and took our seats. We had gotten there plenty early to get the best seat in the house, after all, this was our little boy. About five minutes before the concert was to get started, Dana noticed that she had forgotten her camera in the car and asked me to step back out and get it. She said that it was in her suitcase.

I rushed out to get it before the concert started. I opened the back hatch on our SUV, unzipped her suitcase, grabbed the camera case in a haste, and dashed back in the church. As I walked back in, some of the people that saw me walk out of the church, recognized me from singing in that area and wanted to speak. I took my time trying to speak to everyone as I made my way back up front to sit with my sweet wife.

I had almost reached Dana when I made eye contact with her. She had the most unusual, surprised look on her face. It was a look of terror. I wondered what was wrong. I wondered if she was upset with me that I was taking so long to get seated with her. She got up and came towards me in a flurry. I wondered why she was so wild eyed. What could it be?

She started towards me with this look like I had never seen. She grabbed me by the arm and grabbed the camera case and hurried towards the exit pulling me with her. What had happened?

When I grabbed the camera case from her suitcase, I had done it so fast and in such a hurry, that I didn't notice that her bra was caught on the case. Yep....there I had been dragging the bra that was caught on the camera case right up the center aisle. I had heard a few people snickering but figured it couldn't be anything to do with me.

To say the least, she was totally humiliated. Both of us were. Everyone in the church knew what was going on but me, which is the way it is most of the time! We did watch the concert, but we didn't come back in the church until the service had started and we sat in the very back. We also left early!

This was not the start of his career, but shortly after this, he began to play at church in the college band and the rest is history. God did give us the desires of our heart concerning our sweet son.

CHAPTER 9

"And my God shall supply all your needs according to His riches in glory by Christ Jesus."

Philippians. 4:19 NKJV

- *"According to His riches in Glory by Christ Jesus"* - Paul knew that God the Father does everything He does through His Son Jesus Christ. Were it not for the atonement, there would be no hope. Were it not for the Redeemer, there would be no atonement. So, it would all happen through Christ Jesus.

Heaven had an inexhaustible ability to supply their needs. Their needs would be met through Christ Jesus' abundant fullness; His possessing all things; His overwhelming abundance.

YOUR NEEDS WILL BE MET THROUGH CHRIST JESUS' ABUNDANT FULLNESS.

It was probably around 6 months after my dad passed away on March 20, 2002, that my mom called and wanted to know if I was interested in my dad's truck. She didn't do anything with any of his stuff for a long time. She just couldn't bring herself to go through his things right away. It was just too hard emotionally. I went down and got dads truck. I was thrilled to get it but more intriguing to me than his truck was his tool box on the back of his truck. It was the diamond checker plated tool box that went across the bed of his truck. It had one big lid on it. As I started going through his tool box, I was amazed at all I found. He had everything you could possibly need in case of emergency.

Of course, all different sizes and shapes of wrenches. He had:

- pliers
- a hammer
- nails
- screws
- screwdriver
- a jack

- tire tool
- log chain
- an extra Radiator hose
- extra belts
- a gallon of coolant
- 2 quarts of oil
- an extra serpentine belt
- old plugs and plug wires
- fuses
- wire cutters
- electrical wire and tape
- extra head and tail light bulbs
- and, oh yeah, a coat hanger **and** duct tape just in case!

Anything you needed while you were off and away from the house or on a back road or on a detour. Also, he knew how to fix the vehicle if it broke down.

Do you realize that God has a tool box in heaven that holds all you will ever need on your detour?

Now, please realize that I am not talking about a literal tool box, but He said all the riches in Heaven would be used to provide my needs.

Do You Need His Presence? Peace? Power?

It matters not what your detour is: cancer, divorce, you've just lost your job, your family just abandoned you, or maybe you've just buried the love of your life or someone very special. God wants to walk with you.

At any time, God can lead you back to the interstate, but in the meantime,

With God's provision, we can enjoy the scenery along the detour!

God wants you to Enter His Presence. God wants you to Enjoy His Peace. God wants you to Experience His Power.

And, He wants you to expect His Provision.

CONCLUSION

Hopefully this book can us help empathize with Paul:

"Don't worry about anything; instead, pray about everything. Tell God what you need, and thank him for all he has done. Then you will experience God's peace, which exceeds anything we can understand. His peace will guard your hearts and minds as you live in Christ Jesus. And now, dear brothers and sisters,

one final thing. Fix your thoughts on what is true, and honorable, and right, and pure, and lovely, and admirable. Think about things that are excellent and worthy of praise. Keep putting into practice all you learned and received from me—everything you heard from me and saw me doing. Then the God of peace will be with you. How I praise the Lord that you are concerned about me again. I know you have always been concerned for me, but you didn't have the chance to help me. Not that I was ever in need, for I have learned how to be content with whatever I have. I know how to live on almost nothing or with everything. I have learned the secret of living in every situation, whether it is with a full stomach or empty, with plenty or little. For I can do everything through Christ, who gives me strength. Even so, you have done well to share with me in my present difficulty. As you know, you Philippians were the only ones who gave me financial help when I first brought you the Good News and then traveled on from Macedonia. No other church did this. Even when I was in Thessalonica you sent help more than once. I don't say this because I want a gift from you. Rather, I want you to receive a reward for your kindness. At the moment I have all I need—and more! I am generously supplied with the gifts you sent me with Epaphroditus. They are a sweet-smelling sacrifice that is acceptable and pleasing to God. And this same God who takes care of me will supply all your needs from his glorious riches, which have been given to us in Christ Jesus."

Philippians 4:6-19 NLT

Father,

Thank you for Who You are
and all You've done.
Thank You for allowing me
to share my heart.
I pray that these words
would have an immediate impact
on all who read them.
I pray that you would lift those
that are down, encourage the discouraged,
and strengthen the weak.
May all who read this be forever
changed by your Words.
In your Holy name we pray,

Amen

If you have never surrendered your life to
Christ, you are missing out on the life God
intended you to live. Believe on Him today!

"But to all who believed him and accepted him, he gave the right to become children of God."

John 1:12 NLT

NOTES

1. https://www.merriam-webster.com/dictionary/content

2. MacLaren's Expositions. http://biblehub.com/commentaries/philippians/4-6.htm

3. Matthew 6:25-34 KJV

4. Barnes' Notes on the Bible. http://biblehub.com/nasb/philippians/4-6.htm

5. Perowne, John. Cambridge Bible for Schools and Colleges. http://biblehub.com/commentaries/cambridge/philippians/4.htm

6. https://www.cmalliance.org/devotions/tozer?id=507

7. https://www.gotquestions.org/God-demand-worship.html

8. Matthew 6:9 NKJV

9. Perowne, John. Cambridge Bible for Schools and Colleges.

10. https://www.gotquestions.org/God-demand-worship.html

11. http://www.goodreads.com/quotes/35269-i-have-so-much-to-do-that-i-shall-spend

12. http://www.quotesbuddy.com/prayer-quotes/true-prayer-is-measured-by-weight-not-by-length/

13. http://www.goodreads.com/quotes/558571-talking-to-men-for-god-is-a-great-thing-but

14. Libray.timlesstruth.org/music/what_a_friend_we_-have_in_Jesus/midi/

15. Adrian Rogers. What Every Christian Ought to Know (Nashville: B&H Publishing Group, 2014) 37. https://books.google.com/

16. Peter Kalellis. Finding God's Presence in Our Life: Faith, Prayer, and Action (Mahwah: Paulist Press, 2016) https://books.google.com/

17. https://www.blueletterbible.org/lang/lexicon/lexi-con.cfm?Strongs=G5485&t=KJV

18. http://web.ccbce.com/multimedia/BLB/Comm/david_guzik/sg/Luk_15.html

19. Gordon Fee. Philippians (Grand Rapids: Wm. B. Eerdmans Publishing, 1995) 176. https://books.google.com/

20. https://www.gotquestions.org/guard-your-heart.html

21. http://www.dictionary.com/browse/re-

22. http://www.dictionary.com/browse/mind?s=t

23. http://www.dictionary.com/browse/peace?s=t

24. http://www.anxietycentre.com/anxiety-statistics-information.shtml

25. http://www.theblaze.com/news/2014/01/17/are-christians-misusing-this-wildly-popular-bible-verse/

26. https://billygraham.org/decision-magazine/february-2011/the-holy-spirit-our-helper/

27. Adrian Rogers. What Every Christian Ought to Know, 185.